15 Jun 1985

For J.K.

[illegible]

The Hero Is Nothing

Some of these poems first appeared in the following magazines: *Boxcar, Hambone, Issue, Sulfur, Temblor.*

Library of Congress Catalogue Card Number: 84-52869
ISBN 0-9614385-0-9
Printed in the United States of America

The text of this book was typeset in Bembo and in Garamond No. 3 Italic by Rock & Jones, San Francisco. Design by Jeanne Jambu, Patricia Koren and Robin Palanker. Printing and Smyth-sewn binding by McNaughton & Gunn, Ann Arbor, Michigan.

1,000 copies of *The Hero Is Nothing* were printed February, 1985, of which 27 are numbered and signed by the author.

Kajun Press
209 Mississippi Street
San Francisco
California 94107

The Hero Is Nothing

Dennis Phillips

KAJUN PRESS
San Francisco

I.

Condition from an Endless Set

Dream of Ocean (With Doors)

This dream riddled with doored openings at night
when you fall overboard no one hears you.
In the morning your scream has cooled and merged.

It would be up to you to float calmly, waiting,
or seek one of the doors,
but then rescuers would find nothing
that would matter your choice more final
than their worst fears.

This dream is a hard test.
It is a dream where you say again and again
"This is not a dream. This is waking.
Only in waking can this be said."
You see a deep channel
and in the pulsing waters doors.

☰

Nobody's own temperature
snow grows on the ground
not as we knew it before
arms are cold the winter
has encrusted twigs and stones
rime of ice on saplings
nobody's temperature alone
has bearing outside its enclosure.

What was it like when you first came here?

☰

Trilogy from a Japanese Lullaby in a Music Box

I.

That we are asleep and not duly asleep but hear this:
The test of bells ringing we measure acutely by whose ears
vibrate in first light, in the minor key of first color.

Minor doesn't portend unimportance, only tone
and tone without reference: sadness without context.

The bells might be soft tines of music boxes the melody
a Japanese lullaby this time waking us.
Sad, simple minor.

That we are asleep (it doesn't matter) no reliable judgment meant
no Cartesian deduction adhered to. That. we. sleeping no
interference between the combinations we want to make.
Ears and eyes exchange functions. This becomes solid.
And it's solidity that we've sought
                                        to avoid by falling asleep.

That we, sleeping, bells, tines' chimes' song minor.
Melody not a given, nor rhyme. Melody only one condition
from an endless set. Not preferable perhaps
easier.

        Asleep if the couch, boat, vehicle rocks
        off each of the possible axes.
        Roll pitch yaw that one view of one first color.
        Open (means awake). View equals Melody.

2.

We end in a trailer and derelict means broken asphalt
encroaching sand, you, I, our faces tightened the heat
derelict.

Something brings panic. Something brings up vestigial hormones
the need to run and yet there's a quiet room, sheltered and locked,
paper on one side derelict scene on the other.

This new phase is lost. New belongings lost.

Inside, the broken talisman. Inside the sand noise we make grinds
rebounds from floor to wall. Hollow sound in, out
on lubricant of cleanliness and repair.

This new phase, rude organizing.

Around the trailer sand on a fractured asphalt slab.
I suddenly become your enemy.

Something brings panic. Something brings panic so strong and stubborn
we get tired, or wait, it's me not you, you're in the trailer
I'm trying to get back in.

And dive down again down to the door
to the asphalt scarf.

We are asleep, no, not asleep but gathered, not touching, in heat.

Why do we repeat this scene? We are safe not captive.
Why come back:
Not because it's pleasant. Not for reward.

3.

If dream,
        disc, alarm
if things immobile if omens,
anniversaries, danger are dismissed
and if "and if" were fossilized, barracked alone along
rows and rows of beds?

    If only seeing part of you
    only isolated parts.

If they won't let you move freely only
slippery through them, if, "If 'if' " is only question, not
proposition then.

Of you sinking. Then, if.

        If I wake from hot napping
        and the dream is too close to the fast blade
        and I see you for a second
        in the cloth of your danger, then.
        If.
If only seeing you.

≡

No directions: walls instead, hills, the memory
of destination.
Where light's constant.
Where rooms filled with artifacts
collect and collect
objects and then other rooms
until large buildings and then cities are formed.

There might be a way
to resign or at least
exit.
We tried the photograph
but nothing seems to work.

☰

History as a Moment of Patriarchy

Strata of cloudy liquid.
Williams hovers below which Williams you ask.

Light, imported (from where irrelevant) in tubes
to be used for sudden illumination under ledges
or between the positives of crevice.

A boy and his dog, somewhere beyond Williams
in a protein too injurious to risk.

The light is used. A sound has been detected.
Proper procedure dictates special behavior which
is not feasible. Light is employed to search out the source.

Companion, rest stop, director, passive viewer,
passenger, bread mate, dark sonnet,
lemmings tail us we must be cautious.
Below are the presences of our past
a well we draw from but
an impulse to be thwarted impinges on us.

The obsession with seeing below to them
thrills us.

The light of the world is uncontained, filters down
through abstract layers
from an unquenchable constant explosion
onto the surfaces of porcelain or grey moorings;
is silver and even, falls like a blanket
ignorant of its past.

≡

This would be pleasure not panic
water on the palm the pressure, forward movement.
                    Green bottom an horizon a bluerizon
jinxed a catcall the audience yells out
          “Call the sick one. You asshole, call her.”
Jinxed a particular particular. “Certain gombeen man” just
distraction. “But I’ve got water on the palm,” you cry.

≡

My den of so many murmurs
so many mordants.

My den of many murders
(bow the head).

We are quiet.
Quiescence overwhelms the round light less
reflection more absorption this
the only quality of this
my den.

No one has died here.

We are
at this moment
the rock of air
pulled in after the cyclone we pursue
to seal off the den.

☰

So arid the upstairs an
empty room so arid outside
no car parts but rust. Stark humidity.

Who comprises the contents of these upstairs rooms a
bare floor tells us nothing the laundry strung out
tells us nothing.

O you precarious unaffected upstairs.
We saw you walking out in the handclasp of an olderman
but we can prove nothing.

An old man not an olderman. A grandpa
holding your white hand your dark skin hidden not
to shock him, aged paramour.

So arid upstairs. So blank.
Can I come up here to ask, to see who governs?

≡

It would be like going under
and finding air at the bottom. Like looking up
and seeing the surface far above.
Like seeing the sister of your first lover,
asking her for information which she cannot give.

≡

You were the one I knew long ago still young skin
still seamless, smooth, water tight.

I was around you and your arms a wind on me my ears
against you hollow you hollow on me a rounded, firm, proud

the way you naked are in me an island.

☰

Someone was supposed to fetch you but no one came.
You walk in lost and angered.

You kept waiting to hear steps or calls.
You held out a card for searchers

thought: A blackboard, school chairs,
          the pitted floor, Windows! There aren't any windows.

≡

This doldrum,
road,
tangle of platforms called nimbus.

You don't see this now you
threaten to leave the memory of your cold husk discovered.

And won't be reached.

This doldrum,
stark season.

☰

The showers
with all those
onlookers
                    business a
fact no restraint no
modesty just
violent vomiting
recurrent fever
poison gas

Later
          the desert mountains
          expectation and duty
          replace illness
without towels:
water as shawl

The notion
that on these mountains
the girls in the shower room
crawled up as starfish
glazed in saline

≡

This soon above spring a long a sandbar we'll
call it approach to the place we've waited for avoided a
sacrifice-worthy thing a clear and sudden island whose distance
is only a factor of visibility and openness we
wonder why the channel they've waited so long for said
is so difficult now seems so placid.

☰

That Heat and Blood Are Related

The waters are cleared
        to the bottom of this puddle
        the blood settled, still
on silt.

The age of weaponry not
meant to teach regimental heraldry.

We will speak of fire, of fluid.
But we have no reasons.

        My clear pool
            warm but not alarming.
        The small chamber to transport me
            unseeing to another field refined, made primal.

The water hole
          in no place tactical.

My tears feel hot. They burn me.
But I wipe only clear fluid.

Don't tell me what I have to breach
to find the blood.

☰

Two Angles on Self-Deprecation

He would say later
about her hips
or about the line of belt resting on her hips
or about the ridgepole of her pelvis
he would say, about that section
he dreamed of, stopped working because of,
later, he would say.

Normal advice is heard and considered.
A salute to a landscape that appears in dreams
but won't become solid in memory. Normal. As if quantity.

That her hips held him
fixed, transfixed.
He'd say that all hormones and instinct
were summarized in one curve of flesh.

Not absent perhaps misperceived. A quartet of missing notes.
But the music was scored for solo instrument.
How democracy is lost. As if quantity.

He would say later, about her hips, about how they stirred him.
He would recall a feeling of moot protest, product of obsession. As if.

If he could find her, but it's written solo
only her, part for hips. "I think I'm ugly,"
she'd say, remembering a scene not related but tenacious
so that during all crucial moments, when answers

decisions, commitment must be made,
the image of a long blue pool surrounded by starlets and gigolos,
with summer waiters attending in short white coats,
with no shade anywhere, with the very faint
smell of chlorine and the dissipated arctic of really good
air conditioning
                    would grasp her mind.

She would wonder later why she was the prisoner
of a hotel she had never seen.

Landscape

This
        peculiar combination the
        right streets wrong streets
tread (trepidation) lightly a
                    yellow mar
              tarnishes forward momentum.

The landscape is a control.

              I'll hold you down because you are too buoyant because
              each time the scene I want you to notice comes by
              you are bobbing above it, out of view.

        A scuff of yellow. A mar
        on the well-tended surface.

If one stays away too long the membrane of landscape grows tough.
You say the bobbing from details is a stropping to keen you
to enblade you to lightly slice the membrane.

Membrane of landscape the apparent visual of where we are the
control of what happens not the control that events and things
are regulated but the control that things, events are measured this
control is only backdrop, tempera paint and clever lighting:
all scaffolding that must be broken down if the next membrane true yellow

mar of your sharp attention is to be placed are to be positioned.

*

Only the passage or gesture.

Tank emptied the
species spread out flat
suspension tossed.

As if breath taken deeply in and released in crescendo
were not the completed structure but the essential element.

Water is another.
The living things in it
without it dead.
Breath gone.
Paradox to terrestrials.

Essential element the motor of death.

No vessels to pierce.

Passage would not *mean* anything.

☰

Air Absent

First concrete then nerve ends
   You won't
                  apprehend this:
of you not me. Your news not news.

Without your face this is easy.
Unlooked for parsecs, fences I ask for protection
but in the wrong person.

☰

And then the yellow feathered heart taker
offers you the new one rejection of tissue not
not being scared only not caring that you're on the razor
as you feel the seam against your sternum popping open
the last time it was stone knife on the graduated pyramid
the idea (have they no shame) that one hollow muscle would
prevent rain or cause rain or bring just the right amount of rain
as the taker holds your heart above his head his chin
pointing upward toward the dragon snake eagle savior god
ready to drink but truly expecting
variable cloudiness, a chance of showers, rain for the people
a lack of royal young.

☰

Lance ridden, we mark a collision.
The human voice instrument today.

The air is thick in a way never known.

Heated fragments of summer arrive. Students misuse "attributes" for "contributes." A call comes in: a mansion, an afternoon of idleness. We worship relaxation.

We cannot comprehend time.
Years countable and recent slot into numerical distance.

☰

Three-Part Requiem

Somewhere an image comes clear I
recall the grains of wood thinking of this
driving rain but
can't come up with the scene.

Not Uncle Milton 48 hours dead, sitting in the cab of a pickup truck
already buried, eviscerated and still
on the road sitting white and straightforward
in the cab of this truck I
watch him hoping "Heavenly Car" but that scene too
is an island.

I rise. Cat vomit my own
incontinence dripping this scene
an island.

There are one-hundredfold reasons
called Heavenly Cars, called On the Road
to Islands, called What Drips.

I am sitting on the terminator
of a great umbra.
            My shoulder has tensed into cramp
            locking against my ear
      as if

quoting this scene makes it real.

*

Bloodless uncle fugit.
No guess, the arcane ology.
Taken along or left silent behind?
No reminder late
in a temporal portal
of how briefly the witnessing was permitted
or how sorrowful, forgotten, studied
the fragments.

*

Funeral.   Rain.
                    Dim man pressed
into earth.

☰

Or in truth
    my ardor
            the hemoglobin of lusts
    newspaper or
          how to sound appropriately mad
to evidence depth.
                    The above should remain part of this
                    it is the detritus to be dived through
                    a surface for the diver
            a fabric
of place by the ocean
supported in the centre
by views of a childhood
that may now be judged
too sedate.
    Adolescence in Tahiti
on the turquoise reefs
turquoise stone from deserts
used to refer to tropical seas
a lemon comes into it
because lemons grow near to *this*
this paper, now,
not later or elsewhere,
but here, near the lemons
under the weight of recollected vistas
the childhood that makes slow copy
the childhood that has only minor evidence

but from which terror or anger
emerge

a quiet page now
saddened by what has led to it
too obsessed by its texture and detail
to usually rage.

☰

Unfinished overture. This is tragedy. Cut off.
In the prime. You know the rest. What looks like permanence
chokes off just under way.

On the wayward side of spheres on the
ocean side of islands on the road to Mandalay.
No open oracle.
What we expect to be consular is nemesis.

Marks all over your face and hands.
We are bruised and strained. What a pair
alone, decorated.
Each passionate costume hoped to be anchor
and shield.

A cabinet with red handles a Right Whale on seaways we
don't recognize the lanes the bright overcoat is missing we notice
hardness the sea lacks a surface hardness seems female despite Greek
patronage.

Head moves hair away a missile leaves its underwing last time
you touched yourself the onlookers puked last meal to train time
harps and flutes seem saccharine fizzing up from the bottom of white
tea china small tablets released by an old woman harpless and fluteless.

What small pleasure to ask a globe for rest.

This life alone verified by temporal things and by a whispering whimper a
name called out against background noise a name that sounds like mine
that makes me shut off the water then turn off the heater to
look for quiet to hear the name makes me stop the radio go outside
to the neighbors and theirs to shut off televisions and on to the distant
freeway to stop traffic calming dogs along the way all to cause
silence to hear the whisper to know the name.

☰

Zone

If, now that I come to you a maiden no less than open
my part in a crawl for mercy knees scraped ten miles to the virgins'
toilet three yards of gutter to wade in to crash the bike in If
when I come I come to you as myself it's now that I
listen, hold you across my palms, blank, both of us, tastes like you
do paper and skin, I come to you paper and skin the hope of sanctuary
like birds only I can *remember* you and I can think about you
a maiden no less than your openness and my intrusiveness
to track across you the brink open sanctuary
my most simple waiting battling field.

☰

Ease of dovetail.
Eerie the legs of centipede on your lips.

Telltale. This landscape, these appropriations.
The lasting, the damaged.

What lists remind us of or remand us
  to the obligation or custody of
  daily ritual or its contrived opposite?

Final remembered vista: Head on, invisible;
  seen clearly askance.

≡

Self-Portrait

You. Your attentions. What others say in empty halls
of no concern but where's your recompense Do
they recall your fine manner or deft art in the conferences. Where
are you when these things happen?

So detailed attention to the effects of doors, rain, ocean
there *can* be a debate inside you.

Roughness and electrical affinity may mark your hovering what
else would concern you?

*

You rain-procuring mercenary whose *true* claim we disbelieve.
Dracaena stump expected to blossom tropical in a water jar
on your oak desk the structure of which
conjecture causes your anxiety to see a poor cat
legless, placed in a thimble, faced toward a window that
views fern forest, to wait and look as if you saw
some other significance in so pathetic a scene
as if it were ungenuine, too soft against the rock-hard
vision you seek and so include various hardware
and a backdrop of urbane holidays in tropical settings.

*

You ask why you can't simply make beautiful things the
world you're capable of invoking in itself is moving and then

you become restless and picture the wingbeats and accompaniment
of *Sunday Morning* and know the answer and settle again
for what you demanded or were handed or
what always comes up there's no way of ensuring a result
or a conversation later you'll probably not hear it
or the alternative (you fancy eavesdropping after death) of hearing
them talk about you would be in the context of a world that must
negate the thrill of being remembered.

*

If the picture of cord and rope comes into this it's with
a sense of release not bondage as though
the twisting structure of rope or cord were a pathway not
a prison and if Wittgenstein says that philosophy
must be as complex as the knots it seeks to unravel
then poetry must be a knot, beautiful and impossible
that instead of needing to be untangled,
of its own accord blooms.

☰

Or of the temporality.
Twelve (or was it ten) tasks to avenge guilt.
(Certain reference always sounds classical.)

An information. The name of treading with exact diplomacy.
Nothing left vulnerable, everything covered, but nothing risked.
Where this core stops.

Or a temporal nature.
The uphill park near the dirty motorway.
The headache of a child so severe
the day of it remembered for twenty-five years.

A fact distorted now idea fights with image for place.

≡

And hear "Will-o'-the-wisp"
  tangles this way:
    Cankered, tangible
    smoke becomes relic
    tangles fly to some great undoer.

Speed in these operations crucial to the outcome,
although speed is sometimes fatal
but then the outcome crucially demands
a mortal result.

Example: The face greeting your face
  at *the* door (what door?)
  in rain.

Example: You have presented a calm
  benevolent visage how
  shocked (do you suppose?)
  they'll be when you can't hold it in anymore
  and tear down the chandelier
  due to provocation they hadn't intended
  or to the type of insult they had grown to expect you
  to thank them for.

☰

This brink opposed to planets
lined up electrical currents
pass from eye to eye the
mystery of the succession of things
holds a gravity special to the alignment
not only spatial but molecular
What point could manifest the
specific gravity chilling unpredictable
moved by currents affected by seasons
polar caps restoring bulk from water
lined up perfectly as crystals and in them
a synchronos so that once
in every span of time too impossible to catalogue
all matter forms a straight line and disappears.

☰

Appropriately modest. Ladies-in-waiting flanking you
at nausea's border, at stark tropical lot.
A mystery of body its surprise the declension of your parts
into verbs and prepositions.
This secret is not airtight: Your fantasy of my arrival:
My knowing your number but lacking the fingers to dial.

☰

What I hid today
through a slit I found
in what we thought was a perfect carpet.

There's this emptiness not a bad emptiness
but quiet, absorbing, only receptive.

At a place near the end of highways
where mountains protect a sloping valley
where I expect to be impressed by sheerness
a grey mist erases expectation.

For a moment nothing is left.
A perfect hiding place
more complete, less dirty than Underworld
but transient, unpossessive.

☰

Peninsula

We hear a death cry coming through the earth.
Fine needles, distant, horribly still.
No one will help them. We try to reach
through the earth. Our arms, buried, freeze us to listen.

☰

                  The angel
no less benevolent

            but instead
            we fear it

Beauty and terror seem separate
The shocking coolness of the dead

            ☰

II.

Permission

Themes and Variations

Or if you sleep and I watch you
a hidden narration like a ribbon
decorating the background.

That hill in a wooded country where
one person follows another up a narrow path
the trees bare, a single way to an empty
room where the same travelers
avoid contact.

Instead of a floor a set of steps.

And think of a small core of black diamond
lodged in me where a swallow or
peristalsis, scream or nightmare cannot
dislodge it.

Dredging up an old bottom,
words infused with contrition
fold under but twitch through
a memory of reaching.

*

In the background helicopter orbiting a target
hidden in its narration or explain this
a spotlight follows fugitives over fences

but the wave of sound is not pursuant.

A tiny word-voice peeps out of a permeable membrane,
a sleeping set of vocal organs still looking.
With nails and hair, voice continues to grow
post-mortem.

And then silence, chopped upon, but then only quiet.

And quiet is a recurrent room. Mismanaged time it turns out.
A set of misused figures first thought human
then understood as Cobol or Fortran,
Missionary Waltz or Missile Silo.
No one would guess Beethoven's Fifth.

Music that could be stirred up to float separate
from silt and gravel, raked through by itinerant
grappling hooks which come up empty
and so each new time more likely.

*

Because among other memories are these scenes.
Maybe persistence equates with lack of resolve.
A minute away, wind music without wind.
Or decorating the area near paper, hoping
for a tincture of specific atmosphere.

Adolescence in bed sweet skins in cottons.
First unsolved touches continuous.

There are eyes, words, certain woods and rooms.

Persistent scenes that accumulate
around a knot or gem stuck in my middle.
Congratulations to Laser Science and Computerized Axial Tomography.
O how I know this.

Checking into a certain kind of hospital
to confirm the scenes. And there
see that one kind of surrender occurs
only for relief and protection
but it is not understood or controlled:
Terminal despite volition.

*

Instead of a floor a set of steps. And then silence,
chopped upon, but then only quiet. There are eyes,
words, certain woods and rooms.

A ribbon since childhood tied into knots, the color
crushed red to purple like rose petals
burst on the hollow of a fist.

Narration is invasive, but its malignancy is doubtful.
Is it a fixed tumor or the endometrium making its way to the brain.

A brain surrounded by womb, postpartum and post-mortem.

If I close my eyes a set of voices begins. Their language

is not repeatable its density such that it can't be recalled
even moments after it is heard. Sometimes several come
in voice over, streamers above or through images of silt
or landscapes, woods with narrow paths, groups
of strangers who will not speak.

Hold open a flesh hole, all archeologists here.
Watching the ribbon unwind in your breathing,
being enveloped by the illusion that apparent peace
and verified beauty are the proof against malignancy.

*

Handfuls of sand dropped in clear still water
first the sound it makes then the cloud it makes.

Narration without image; image without narrative.
While you sleep the shell but also the personae
between us, speaking, play roles
of significance only once,
in a moment, under glass.
I'm relieved to find only you when I return.

The dialogues like pennants, explanations like anvils.

Your voice comes out nocturnal hunter. A grappling
sound searching for quarry. Bundle of empty tines.
Or I'll tie you into my own confusion with a counterpoint,
answers to your questions which belong on but evade your hooks.

What I see is in negative, layers on layers:
at first an argument of style but later
family a matrix of behaviors
all concerned with not continuity but continuing.
The fine old tellers are dead. We keep the images.

*

Very little lodges in me my throat must be smooth inside
or I seem to wait for something that will not lodge.
Only one thing, black and solid. Under my Xiphoid Process.
And from there into my lungs and blood.
There is no meterology in this lump of diamond.
It is constant, intractable: Carbon.

You're asleep now and I am on a moving board
called weekdays for which you should rest.
I picture your place there
but not the order of events. Because here while you're gone
the craziest things happen and when I look down it's an
androgynous pallet, I'm not here, your arms, words' mercy,
my dumb knot.

A marshal ribbon, slogan and polish. And no camouflage.

I crawl into a coat of sand
tight and locked the words So and Then
among the vanquished. Permission to use the arms denied.
The word lists extended.

Or on all fours retching up fluid but nothing solid.
It seems that resolve to continue and surrender
are synonymous. Sinister tines circle like bats.
The ribbon now mummifies me with sand mortar.
"The rules," I yell. "The rules."
But should have begged *remission*.

≡

If you want to sleep and I, the only one left on earth,
sit under one light the words are moving no sleep interrupts I'm
not away from you but alone with music. Words
don't rid the soul.

☰

With heat comes emptiness.
    Tacit quiet.
                Pollution wets the fire.
                Heat without burning.

The equilibrium too effective.

Doors slam on both sides.
The house in heat surrounded by exit.

Pelts excessive, spread out close to the coolest.
Heavy things settle like stirred silt remembering a bed.

☰

We fall to the underworld by choice.
Smaller and smaller details beckon.
Their voices imagined, finite.
We cannot retrieve lost things.

But insoluble darkness
drinks light and sound and touch,
pulls us to its shore.

We arrive without offerings
for the voices awaiting blood.

We bring only heat
which rises back to overworld.

No voice greets us.
Nothing is received.

☰

Because I'm lunar the circle the track I
take my disc talk from umbra
full umbrage to the Canon of Silver.

And the course
to the words
disc.

Language won't reach around.

Shadow must be followed. Its course
marked more carefully. Its voice
simple. The blood comes up with this
accounting of blood moves the umbra
over our landscape. *When I Decided To*
Use We is crawled over
by red dark.

☰

In the red dress on
          stairs
                in the robe red
          backstage

     a vibrato
     or a song
     we don't agree on

Gulf of age or skin or money

The red shimmer
          the young guards
                who hold you.

I have the number, access, illusion
of how to get through.

How well the sound will carry
quavering, controlled and high.

          Your whisper
          I hear.

≡

The Name of Polybus's Queen

Don't. In this glade. Beside a box we found
feign birth. We know the ruse.

Let's instead of the box
                    open something softer:
Obsession is softer. Obsession conforms to all shapes and angles.
Suddenly obsession blanks the faces
nulls the voices, makes things hard
but sometimes numb.

Rumor has it that the box contained a child.

So take me to the white house.

In the white house we have discovered the secret cache
of rare wine which we may not touch. We
have implanted ourselves in a small loft
because in the half-moon light white walls
weaken to us.

A public demonstration only confuses matters.

My warning to you is needless, I know. That *was*
you on the beach of river and ocean.
I did see you, didn't I, carefully pounding the box
into splinters, the name of your husband on each slat?

Your child is safe.

☰

What I made nonsense
        a weed spire rises
I call for the honey-sweet wine,
control my lip and covet.
Stop me. The full demon moon,
my fingers, my fangs.
Possessions obsess me.

You fill me with perfume and fine aristocratic skin.

Or you are different, angelic
fill me with your eyes
your voice, your blood, your pulse.

Lights dim and repower.
Little girls offer favors behind sleeping boyhusbands.
My only possession is chaos.

≡

Sound subsides.

Your face rises
from some nonspecific blank
and I can feel it here.

A storm passes prematurely.
The ocean churns up, splashes over the sides.

This time listen. Water seeps in around us.
Your voice is now a solid thing in the palm of my hand.
A guardian, you think, and wait to speak.

☰

In my room.
        Don't tell me.
About the fortress in a single spire.

A great rock anchor in the room
temporarily displaced, deployed elsewhere.

Instead I take the bowl of smoke
keeping the blue pilot flame alive with my slowness.

They will stall and ask and deny
this room, then, is detached.
Leave a lot of tape I may need to speak.
Leave the key to the zip of your skin,
I'll invent an exit.

☰

We couldn't know (tell) whose month it was. Our
sequestered float without calendar.
The complex theory we had collaborated on
about sync, matches, ties: worthless, laughable.

Thus: It is early. It is 3 or 4 AM. After an overture
of thin metal quieted, you're at the window.
"Dogs," you say.

Hence: Rising beyond a newly seen vista
of Mojave desert is the imagined denture of the southern
Sierras. We fly past them,
turn east, to the third valley.

You speak to the window spirits we
bring to that moment an expectation. And yet
a powerful hook holds us down, separate.

☰

Mouths open on each other, disqualified.
The smell then taste of blood.

Laden corners
where we could not hide.
Our notion of seclusion
becoming more particular
so that public spots are considered
avoiding postures we can't abide
in private.

I'm not surprised
when your touch leads to a kiss.

But there's no tongue in your mouth
only air, warm air.

There is no apology in your face
no hint that something is wrong.
Perhaps nothing is wrong.

☰

I sat on a bleached plain we talk about moods,
alleviation, the back of my head, a knot of capillaries
where caffeine is caught where headache
is fertilized in tight cords.

    Nor touch even your hand,
    rounded digits forgotten.

A specific of civilization.

    From a netted root ball
    Medulla Oblongata,
    a water basin rimmed
    a chance to drink.
    One hundred canceled tributaries.

Our porcelain desert.

≡

Resting what words come come on my face
now my hands are full or useless my face
holds words now my scorpion babies crawl
in the wet white hairs.

Rain comes rain won't cease rain
pries into everything nothing
dry no watertight seal without seepage.

But hold me still a rash of doors
bursts from legs and belly.
Even my useless nipples open to purge.
The babies still too small to turn.

The name comes over me.
Stings and cuticles. O permission givers.

☰

All the time wondering you ask whereabouts.

I ask you, regarding gibbous moon, to speak of
dim light, the women Colleen, dogs which had been.

Looking in a silver light.

Wondering your whereabouts. Asking
debutante dancers to quit the baboon
to pause in aid to a guest.

Permission a burning theme.
Where some would take this apart.

One small word I ask for one small word.
At a time. When permission grows in value.
And we arm in silver.

☰

When your voice clears static.
But what poem came to me in my dream too
sad to bring out with me I'm
relieved to hear you I am relieved
to feel my name in your mouth

"I am Hitler" it read "I have
run out of babies to smother."
But the first line is gone.
Questions were asked of me
I held several bundles in my arms.

Please forgive me but the answers have fled.

Thank you for retrieving my ordinary name.

☰

Nobility, gait: tell me. Open this speech
conveyor belt: my landscape. Weeping
attached against my will. To: island of birds
island of enchantresses: singular.

But I was too busy spitting up. O, my bib got dirty
my work went wrong. All I could hear
were castanets, a chorus of altos.

I remember the boiling down of blood. And was
so contrite: only returned when fire
had set it all out. An unusable crust remaining.
My mirage. Weeping in birdland. What was
conjured, I alone, the brave new birds.

Hold the center, I call out menaced.
Sunless sea.

≡

We are standing at the nexus
with the morons or demons of politics
counting our pulse on one side
the abyss of neglect or sabotage
on the other.

It seems that we can breathe underwater
but we know that's part of the plan to fool us.

Xs on our mouths we steam under bindings.

The view is perfect. We see them
getting butt-fucked with warheads, laughing
from straightened mouths.

Chalk like gymnasts use. Like
a subcontinent casually turned from solid
to powder. That's not applause, it's disposal.

☰

A face I plead with from the distant past
agrees now, solved, brings roses
on a long climb, ladder by ladder
to the peak of all roofs
a chasm of yellow and pink flutters petals confetti
all the way down.

Next to me a body I remember from hours ago
in a T-shirt that recent
change from hello to goodnight, corsage
on her bosom, pleasantry, ceremonial
orchid offset by roseleaf.

Say yes, I tell them. Say what they want to hear.
Soil over the clean petals
ladder by ladder to the heavenly halls
as shields but strewn on the way up
where Polyphemus awaits a new eyelid
and is soothed to take soft petals and lay them over
his singed, dried scar.

But it's in a car where the face agrees.
And succumbs my
wish her wish, but here, in rosewater ink.

*

Disappear me a crescent shape and we panic

the teller gave us Cairo and religious fanaticism.
We will try to confess this in Egyptian or
hold up a newspaper to shield responses.
Signatures less important, we've mentioned the
fickle ink.

Suddenly an entire serving class leaves work to pray.
We have determined that we are invulnerable
to causes we had once feared.

The poor houses left uncared for.
The streets of Rosetta
trying to figure the reasons or puzzle
the reactions.

The corsage on your arab dress
has not been trimmed.
Roses blossom from your face
your neck. The sharp stems
pierce your nervous skin.
A prison grows around us,
warnings ignored.

☰

It was a religious face or a face from romance.
It was an erotic face giving a tongue tip
to your lips. It was a religious face
and the response was violent.

The cork won't fit back in.

Not in the name of Eros nor Aphrodite.
The flowers were decoys. But a horrible name
without vowels sucks out your will.

≡

Later it will be impossible to move simple objects.
An envelope in front will not make sense.
The time ladder splits into teeth that
mesh as gears against each other.

A jew inherits the canon.

Buildings disconnect, halls become land tracts.
Ordinates are benevolent; time not.

I've forgotten to wear my shoes. The paycheck drops
but the envelope closes my eyes. If I try to replace them
my interest will seem like treachery.

Elpenor reaches in, attached but vanquished.

Small amber cubes, sharp cubes clog his ears.
We borrow Elpenor today, we like him
partially deaf. We have no reason to give him
all he wants is a proper fire.
We borrow matches to console him.

The hero is nothing.

From limbo we are given a new vine
its leaves are furry, its casings burst
with orange flowers. They will burn completely
but only at the right moment, by the right corpse.

☰

Then find it
barren as always.

A minuscule change, angle of light,
that's all. I would stop here.
I would stop and wait for recall.
Instead I salmon up this dry bed some
instinctual pool calling me but arid
I slap down on hot boulders, belly over, push
against air.

At the pool Persephone is laughing.
She opens a red fruit:
it's filled with fish eyes.
"You're here anyway," she says.

☰

There must be a reason for the tropical it offsets the
inside dry and caked. Or I presume.

A state of light, new verb,
where the sun hits tired trees
hot against black cloud.

When rain stops
and heat returns.

Then crack it open.
Inside is dry sand,
hot, hard clay.

We come to a land
that has no shade.
The world does not exist.

☰

There is a face and I've disarmed it
another face grows behind I
alarm it to me.

Far off keys chime.
The skin itself holds certain secrets. Its
sensitive receptors.

Repeating what you have learned and understood is obscene.

Our envelope: the skin.
A face I conjure, a face I cancel.
Bone and tears, warmth.

Keys are presented. They do not fit.

The faces in my hands
look at me, see themselves held.
They are not created, they do not die
in my hands.

☰

Valediction

I'll try you. A marble sweater. A cold water.
A cabin in some obscure mountain range.
I'll speak up.
The sounds of this dark city are productions
in color, with audience. I'll be here but
awake in the muggy heat or sleep
so completely that I won't be here.

We will percolate something not yet found
through the crudest shapes and matter.
I can hear someone singing from a
production: The music the voices,
they will be part of the silt layer.

Old age forces the hand to narrative.
It is an hour when we normally would speak.
So I'll remember your body in water
I'll count you, as if you were many pieces.

We race through dark streets
shadows on shadows, quiet, fast, cool.
We are alone. We breathe a pure element
and conjure something, try all night to bring it
and then want release.

The filter's top layer is marble: slabs, stones,
busts, cloth.

But you are in blue, cold because it's

far away. But sharp and
if I hold onto it, it takes me

into a clean blue, where you are, a
series of photos instead of history, a
song, a sweater, a rubber cap.
And then, as if we held our breath,
we obsess with gravity, suspending it
and the song and the voices
are gone. The photos have melted back into liquid.

We are sent through and halfway can't escape:
We exhale; things dropped fall.
We're sent through but for the longest time
linger on the floe of marble.
It isn't cold. We seem to float unquestionably
we seem to float.

And race through a dark street, the neighbors are sleeping
but we are awake. I'll try you now.
We have conjured or found something.
We watch it: Will it fall up or down. Will it
collapse deflated or melt back into liquid?

☰

I close my eyes
they skin
a zebra.

Three of me now
three of them, pulling inside
out, one piece, perfect.

Although there is a narrator
I know we have been
constantly, are always, here.

☰

It is 3 o'clock the window is white the light grey
the breeze has begun as usual. By 7 o'clock
the air will be still, the window rosy, Homeric.
At 8 o'clock 100 years ago? I can't
tell. If I drill this spot I still won't find
layered wind or light.

A year from now I won't find you
unless I search.

☰

A rain not a rain. That I take this
ready to stop. A second time. A moment
all other moments have led to.

Bristles. Combed up, against grain against daylight.
From space an eddy of cloud a silent concussion.

An atom is bombarded. These cells are burned.
They bristle up in fear.

A single strand waits where a double was used.
A cry, held up in a tubular tissue. A rain
not a rain a release of one into another.
A larder depleted and filled again. My closet
revealed as empty. My closest catalogue
typed and rowed. Money a vanished crest
on a junior blazer.

I arrive at the point again willing.
But not in the same way. How?
I don't answer that I don't know how I answer
with a reef somewhere a shallow reef stretching
out to an horizon until lately I've been
home and stubborn, quiet and paralyzed.

I can sleep to this sound now to this
silent blind of white and muffled thunder not thunder
rain but a roof now under stood. Finally.

☰

One card floats ashore.

☰